WHY CHOOSE JUDAISM:
New Dimensions of Jewish Outreach

David Belin

Union of American Hebrew Congregations
New York, New York

SPECIAL BIENNIAL DEDICATION

Presentation of this gift volume to delegates to the 1987 UAHC General Assembly was made possible through a generous grant from the UAHC Connie Belin Memorial Fund.

Connie Belin loved Jewish education and the UAHC Outreach Program, chaired since its inception by her husband, David. She shared his dream of a vibrant North American community of ever-increasing numbers who would understand that the central benefit of Jewish Outreach is the impact of Judaism on the life of the individual in terms of learning, worship, personal faith, and happiness and in terms of the values and deeds by which women and men conduct their lives.

Her memory and her legacy will forever be a blessing.

I dedicate this booklet to the memory of the six million Jewish women, men, and children who were murdered by the brutal Nazi Regime which attempted to forever extinguish the contributions of the Jewish people to humankind. Fortunately for all of us—both Jews and non-Jews—despite the Nazis and all of their predecessors, Jewish survival has continued and, hopefully, with the catalyst of Jewish Outreach, will continue in the centuries to come.

SPECIAL ACKNOWLEDGEMENTS

The achievements of the Joint Task Force for Reform Jewish Outreach and the Joint Commission for Reform Jewish Outreach, which it has been my privilege to chair since their inception, would not have been possible without all of the help and support given by outstanding lay people and rabbis who are members of the Reform Jewish movement. I could name every member of the Board of Trustees of the Union of American Hebrew Congregations, but in particular I want to mention the great assistance given by the two immediate past Board chairmen, Matthew Ross and Donald Day, and our current chairman, Charles Rothschild, Jr. Our president, Rabbi Alexander Schindler, who has such profound perspective, has played a key role in the overall development and implementation of modern Jewish Outreach, and the entire American Jewish community is indebted to him for his leadership.

I also want to thank those lay people and rabbis who have given so much of their time and talent as members of the Joint Task Force and the current Joint Commission on Reform Jewish Outreach: Rabbi Martin P. Beifield, Jr., Stanley J. Beskind, Harry Davidson, Rabbi Joseph A. Edelheit, Carl Feldman, Shirley Firestein, Rabbi Steven Foster, John A. Geller, Rabbi Joseph Glaser, Roberta Goldman, Samuel P. Goldstein, Rabbi Leslie Y. Gutterman, Dr. Robert Hess, Richard Imershein, Rabbi Walter Jacob, Lee Kahn, Mary Lynn Kotz, Constance Kreshtool, Lydia Kukoff, Rabbi Howard Laibson, Dr. Judith Landau, Seymour M. Liebowitz, Ira Lipman, Rabbi Allen Maller, Lillian Maltzer, Rabbi Bernard Mehlman, Melvin Merians, Rabbi Eugene Mihaly, Lucille Miller, Margery Miller, Josephine Narva, Ruth Nussbaum, Dr. Boris O'Mansky, Rabbi Burton Padoll, Rabbi W. Gunther Plaut, Constance

Reiter, Jocelyn Rudner, Larry Sachnowitz, Rabbi Herman E. Schaalman, Rabbi Robert Schur, Rabbi Sanford Seltzer, Rabbi Max Shapiro, Jane Sherman, Cindy Stein, Elizabeth V. L. Stern, Dr. Melvin Sturman, Rabbi Daniel Syme, Paul Uhlmann, Jr., Rabbi Mark L. Winer, and Rabbi Sheldon Zimmerman.

In particular, Rabbis Max Shapiro and Sheldon Zimmerman, who successively served as Task Force co-chairmen, and Rabbi Steven Foster, who serves as the current co-chairman of the Outreach Commission, have been extremely supportive and helpful in the work of the Task Force and the Commission. Lydia Kukoff, the current director of the Joint Commission on Reform Jewish Outreach, and Rabbi Sanford Seltzer, the original director of the Task Force and the current co-director of the Commission, have done outstanding work in the implementation of the work of the Task Force and Commission. Finally, I want to mention Rabbi Daniel Syme, who has brought to the Commission his tremendous perspective as director of the Department of Education of the Union of American Hebrew Congregations.

The success of the work of the Task Force and the Commission on Outreach would not have been possible without the contributions and support of these wonderful members of the American Jewish community.

Many people have reviewed the manuscript and have made valuable suggestions and constructive criticism. These include:

Milton Brown, Carolyn Bucksbaum, Melva Bucksbaum, Donald S. Day, Marjorie Fisher, Max Fisher, Rabbi Steven Foster, Dr. Robert Hess, Marvin Klass, Mary Lynn Kotz, Lydia Kukoff, Norma U. Levitt, Richard Levitt, Melvin Merians, Dr. Eugene Mihaly, Bernard Rapoport, Matthew Ross, Rabbi Alexander Schindler, Rabbi Sanford Seltzer, Billie Tisch, Laurence Tisch, Dr. Paul Vanek, Rabbi Sheldon Zimmerman.

In addition to their suggestions and criticisms, Dr. Joanne Brown and Rabbi Daniel Syme have spent a great deal of time in helping the editing of the manuscript and I am particularly appreciative of the help they have given me.

David Belin

WHY CHOOSE JUDAISM:
New Dimensions of Jewish Outreach

WHY CHOOSE JUDAISM?

"Why should I choose to be Jewish?" It is a question that is being asked with increased frequency throughout the United States and Canada in a variety of circumstances.

When a Jew and a non-Jew fall in love and decide to marry, the Jew may ask his or her intended spouse to choose Judaism. Why? What is there about the Jewish religion that would lead the non-Jew to want to change religious identity?

The parents of a Jew contemplating marriage to a non-Jew usually want the prospective son-in-law or daughter-in-law to consider converting to Judaism. Why should the non-Jew choose Judaism?

If the non-Jew does not convert to Judaism, in what religion will their children be raised? Why should the couple raise their children to be Jewish?

If a child is not raised in the religion of either parent on the rationale of freedom of choice upon reaching adulthood, the young adult may ask: "Why should I choose the religion of my Jewish parent?"

These questions directly relate to what has come to be known as Jewish Outreach — one of the most challenging developments in modern Jewish history.

Related to this new development is the increasingly large number of Americans today searching for religious identity. Generally speaking, they have not considered the possibility of choosing Judaism because of the erroneous perception by most non-Jews that Judaism is a closed society or that Judaism does not seek to bring others into the Jewish

1

religion. In fact, Jewish Outreach has historic roots going back to biblical times. But even if those roots did not exist, Jews have a moral obligation to let those searching for religious identity know that they have every opportunity, if they so desire, to choose Judaism.

I believe there is a unique opportunity for thoughtful Jews to enhance the quality of their lives by exploring answers to the questions: "Why should I choose to be Jewish?" and "What is Jewish Outreach and what does Jewish Outreach mean for me?" A similar opportunity exists for non-Jews who may be involved in an interfaith relationship with a Jew or who may have no religious preference but are searching for a personally and philosophically satisfying religious affiliation.

Accordingly, this booklet is designed to help a variety of people: those involved romantically in an interfaith relationship; interfaith married couples who have not yet settled on a single religion for themselves or their children; parents or close relatives of the Jewish partner in an interfaith relationship or marriage; unaffiliated Jews of young adult age, including those in college, some of whom are "targets" for cults and many of whom are unaware of Jewish Outreach, the uniqueness of Judaism, and the relevance of Judaism to our daily lives; and non-Jews of no religious preference who may want to gain some insight into Judaism, which might in turn lead to enrollment in an Introduction to Judaism course.

An additional goal of this booklet is to inform Jewish men and women of all ages and backgrounds about the essence of Jewish Outreach, its development, and its crucial importance for Jews and the survival of Judaism.

Finally, you may find that your life and the lives of your family or someone else dear to you may be greatly enhanced through your exploration into the critical questions: "Why should I choose to be Jewish?" and "What is Jewish Outreach and what does Jewish Outreach mean for me?"

PART 1
THE UNIQUENESS
OF JUDAISM

As one begins searching for answers to these questions, it is natural
to ask: "Does Judaism make any difference in the values, attitudes,
and actions of its adherents?" To be sure, there are Jews who are
moral and righteous and there are Jews who are not, just as in the
general population there are Catholics, Protestants, and non-affiliated
people who are moral and righteous and those who are not. Yet, many
people believe that Judaism is unique and, among other things, they
cite differences in the attitudes of Jews in the United States as
compared with the population as a whole.

For instance, why is it that traditionally Jews have had a high
degree of reverence for parents and grandparents and for teachers and
education? Why is it that traditionally Jews have had relatively low
rates of alcoholism, delinquency, and divorce — differences which
unfortunately are lessening as assimilation between the Jewish and the
non-Jewish community increases?[1] To each of these questions there

---

[1] Attitudes of Jews on political issues also show the impact of Judaism. For instance,
a 1984 survey taken among 750 out of more than 2,000 participants in a biennial
conference sponsored by the largest Jewish charitable fundraising agency in the
United States — the United Jewish Appeal — disclosed that only 3 percent favored a
constitutional amendment permitting prayer in public schools and 94 percent
opposed such an amendment. Although Jews individually may not favor abortion
from a personal standpoint, they nevertheless believe in freedom of choice, as
evidenced by the fact that the 1984 survey showed that only 1 percent favored a
constitutional amendment prohibiting abortions and 97 percent were against.

may be multiple answers. But is it not reasonable to assume that at least one of the reasons underlying these differences is the uniqueness of Judaism and the influence of the Jewish religion and culture on Jews?

Most people recognize that there are many values common to both Judaism and Christianity, starting with the "Golden Rule" first presented in Leviticus (the third book of the Jewish Bible), "You shall love your neighbor as yourself." At the same time, major philosophical differences distinguish these two faiths.

Emphasis on Human Actions and Spiritual Merit

Initially, many people say that the most fundamental difference is the belief of Christians in the divinity of Jesus as the Messiah. Jews through the ages have worshiped God. However, they have never worshiped any man or woman and do not believe Jesus to be the Messiah because, among other things, he failed to fulfill the ultimate messianic prophecy of universal peace that "nation shall not lift up sword against nation, nor shall they learn war any more." Nor do Jews believe that any mortal is God.

However, in their book, *Eight Questions People Ask about Judaism*, Dennis Prager and Rabbi Joseph Telushkin assert that:

> Whether or not Jesus was the Messiah is not the most important question which divides Judaism and Christianity.
>
> The major difference between Judaism and Christianity lies in the importance each religion attaches to faith and law. In

---

Seventy-two percent favored government funding to help poor people who want an abortion and 15 percent opposed. On international issues, 85 percent favored a U.S.-Soviet bilateral and verifiable nuclear freeze and 7 percent opposed. Eighty-three percent favored more government spending for education and 2 percent favored less government spending for education.

Judaism man is judged by God by his deeds, not by his faith; according to the Bible, observance of the laws of the Torah [the first five books of the Bible] is the Jews' central obligation. As Christianity developed, however, it did away with biblical law, and consequently faith became its central demand. (Page 71)

A similar perspective is given by Rabbi Abba Hillel Silver in his book, *Where Judaism Differed:*

The Kingdom of God — which mankind with the help of God is to build — is in Judaism's view definitely of this world, and all of man's tasks are centered here. In Judaism, the Kingdom of God means the Good Society. In Christianity, it means the Future World — the Hereafter. (Page 183)

Related to these differences is the Christian doctrine of Original Sin, a concept to which Jews do not adhere. In the words of Rabbi Silver:

In Judaism the soul of man requires no "liberation," because the soul of man is not enchained. The idea that man needs to be "saved" either from the toils of life or from some Original Sin or from the prison house of matter or from baleful astrological influences is not part of Judaism. (Page 183)

Of course, deeds also play an important role in Christianity, just as faith plays an important role in Judaism. Historically, Jews have believed in the existence of a covenant between God and the Jewish people. The Bible says that the Jewish people were chosen by God as the divine instrument for perfecting the world under the kingdom of the Almighty. In the words of Isaiah, "I the Lord have called you for a covenant of the people for a light unto the nations." However, even though the covenant is a part of the tradition of Judaism, because of the priority of the Jewish emphasis on deeds rather than faith, none of the three major branches of Judaism (Orthodox, Conservative, and Reform) asserts that an individual has to have a particular set of beliefs or else be condemned. In the words of Milton Steinberg in his book, *Basic Judaism:*

According to the Tradition, all men, regardless of race, religion, or nationality, are equally God's children, equally precious in His sight, equally entitled to justice and mercy at the hands of their fellows. Except by virtue of character and conduct, no man is better than any other.

Anyone may become a Jew; but no one has to do so in order to be saved, whether in this world or the next.

The Tradition rules explicitly: "The righteous of all peoples have their share in the world-to-come."

On which very consequential point Judaism stands in sharp contrast to historic Christianity. . . .

. . . Judaism holds that any righteous person may expect whatever rewards accrue to righteousness in this world or the next.

Judaism's readiness to recognize that others aside from Jews possess spiritual merit sufficient for salvation constitutes an instance of liberalism almost unique in Western theology. (Pp. 98-100) (Emphasis added.)

This fundamental philosophical concept of Judaism as a religion concerned with deeds permeates Jewish tradition and prayer. For instance, *Pirke Avot (Ethics of the Fathers)*[2], one of the principal writings of Jewish lore, says: "The world is sustained by three things: by Torah, by worship, and by loving deeds." This passage has been incorporated in *Gates of Prayer,* the prayer book of the Reform (or Liberal) branch of Judaism, and it also appears in the prayer books of

---

[2] *Pirke Avot* was written more than 1,500 years ago and has probably been reproduced and reprinted more often than any other talmudic work. Even though the Talmud was written in ancient times, many of its teachings are relevant today. On the other hand, there are many ancient Jewish writings, including portions of the Talmud (and portions of the Bible also), which appear irrelevant or harsh by today's standards, although by the standards of the times in which they were written the laws and commentaries were a great advance over existing systems. A key to appreciating the richness of Jewish religious history and tradition is to put Jewish teaching, writing, and religious laws, such as the Talmud, in the context of their times and to judge them by the standards of those times. One of the major goals of Reform Judaism today is to maintain the highest religious, ethical, and moral standards and guides in the continued growth and development of humanity.

the other two main branches of Judaism. Moreover, the primary importance of human actions and deeds is repeatedly emphasized in religious services. For instance, here are two excerpts from *Gates of Prayer* which contains several alternative Friday evening Shabbat (Sabbath) services.

> May I be blessed on each Shabbat with the sense of having grown in goodness and compassion. There have been times when I endeavored to help those in need. Now I ask only that I may be able to do yet more. Let my actions testify to my worth as Your partner in creation; more and more let me find my life's meaning in working with others to bless our lives by making this a better world. (Shabbat Service II)

> Looking inward, I see that all too often I fail to use time and talent to improve myself and to serve others. And yet there is in me much goodness, and a yearning to use my gifts for the well-being of those around me. This Sabbath calls me to renew my vision, to fulfill the best that is within me. For this I look to God for help.

> Give meaning to my life and substance to my hopes; help me understand those about me and fill me with a desire to serve them. Let me not forget that I depend on others as they depend on me; quicken my heart and hand and lift them up; make fruitful my words of prayer, that they may fulfill themselves in deeds. (Shabbat Service IV)

Emphasis on Study and Learning

Study and learning have also been revered Jewish traditions for thousands of years. In part this has contributed to the traditional Jewish respect for teachers and the emphasis on education. For more than fifteen centuries Jews have read from *Ethics of the Fathers:*

> Joshua ben Perachya: Get yourself a teacher; acquire a friend to

study with you. When you judge people, give them the benefit of the doubt.

Hillel: Do not separate yourself from the community; do not be certain of yourself until the day you die; do not judge another until you are in his position . . . and do not say: "When I have leisure I shall study" — you may never have any leisure.

Yet, even though learning is important in the Jewish tradition, deeds have always been considered even more important. For instance, from *Ethics of the Fathers:*

Rabbi Elazar ben Azarya: When our learning exceeds our deeds we are like trees whose branches are many but whose roots are few: the wind comes and uproots them. . . . But when our deeds exceed our learning we are like trees whose branches are few but whose roots are many, so that, even if all the winds of the world were to come and blow against them, they would be unable to move them.

Emphasis on Freedom

Related to the Jewish emphasis on this world and a person's deeds is the Jewish emphasis on freedom. The oldest continuing annual celebration of freedom in the history of humankind is the festival of Passover. Underlying this traditional concern for freedom is the basic Jewish value of equality among all human beings. In the words of Rabbi Abba Hillel Silver in his book, *Where Judaism Differed:*

Judaism rejected all the caste and race ideologies of the ancient world. Hierarchy has been called an Aryan concept. It is certainly not a Jewish concept. Judaism defied all notions of inherent racial and national superiorities. The prophet Amos made it unmistakably clear to his people: "Are you not like the Ethiopians to Me, O People of Israel? says the Lord. Did I not bring up Israel from the land of Egypt and the Philistines from Caphtor and the Syrians from Kir?"(Amos 9:7) The implications of this verse can be fully grasped only if we recall that the Philistines and Syrians were the traditional enemies of Israel, and the Ethiopians (who were black) were universally despised. Nevertheless the prophet tells his nation that Yahweh is also the God of those nations, that He guides their destinies as well, and in His sight they and Israel are alike. (Page 267)

One of the best illustrations of the concern of Jews for freedom is the great involvement of Jews in organizations seeking to uphold "First Amendment" freedoms, in particular freedom of speech, freedom of the press, and freedom of religion. Another example is the large percentage of Reform and Conservative Jews in favor of the Equal Rights Amendment. (Among Reform Jews, it is estimated that more than 80 percent favor ERA).

The Jewish concern for freedom has been carried into the modern Reform Jewish Shabbat evening synagogue service. For instance, from *Gates of Prayer:*

Lord, we give thanks for the freedom that is ours, and we pray for those in other lands who are persecuted and oppressed. Help them to bear their burdens, and keep alive in them the love of freedom and the hope of deliverance. (Service V)

These Sabbath candles are symbols of the holiness we seek.

Their brightness dispels gloom and lights a path to faith and hope.

Their glow reminds us of the sacred bonds that link us to our people over space and time.

Their radiance summons us to fulfill our people's mission:

To cast the light of freedom, justice, and peace upon all the world. (Service VII)

Respect for Parents
and Emphasis on Family

Jewish tradition has always emphasized the family and, in particular, reverence and respect of children for parents.

Traditionally, Jewish parents have sacrificed much to create greater opportunity for their children. There are the stories of "my son, the doctor" or "my son, the lawyer" (which more accurately today might be "my daughter, the doctor"; "my daughter, the lawyer"). At the same time, Jewish children have always emphasized the responsibility of taking care of their parents. Thus, there is the story of the non-Jewish couple who sought to adopt a Jewish child because they had always heard that Jewish children take care of their parents in their old age.

Perhaps the most personal prayer in the Jewish worship service is the Kaddish — a prayer that extolls God and is said by mourners who reaffirm their belief in God even though they are in grief. Traditionally, it is said by mourners during the mourning period or on the anniversary of the death of a parent or other member of one's family. The Kaddish itself binds one generation to the next and plays an important role in instilling reverence for parents, even after they are no longer living.

Among the most moving meditations in *Gates of Prayer* are optional selections to be read immediately before the Kaddish. The very first of these exemplifies the importance of family relations in Judaism as well as the beauty of Jewish tradition:

> The origins of the Kaddish are mysterious; angels are said to have brought it down from heaven. . . .
>
> It possesses wonderful power. Truly, if there is any bond strong enough to chain heaven to earth, it is this prayer. It keeps the living together and forms a bridge to the mysterious realm of the dead. One might also say that this prayer is the . . . guardian of its continuance. Can a people disappear and be annihilated so long as a child remembers its parents?
>
> Because this prayer does not acknowledge death, because it

permits the blossom, which has fallen from the tree of humankind, to flower and develop again in the human heart, therefore it possesses sanctifying power.

The involvement of family is central to Jewish tradition. Nowhere is this more evident than the Shabbat evening dinner where candles are traditionally lit and blessings are recited or chanted over wine and bread. The fact that the Jewish religion encompasses in large measure home participation is very unique, and it has undoubtedly played a central role in enriching the relationships between husbands and wives and parents and children. There is a well-known phrase, "As Israel has kept the Sabbath, so the Sabbath has kept Israel." In a sense, one can adapt this and say, "As the Jewish family has participated in Sabbath tradition, so has Sabbath tradition helped maintain the Jewish family."

The observance of important religious holy days, which includes family participation in the home such as the dinner on the Jewish new year (Rosh Hashanah), the pre-fast and breaking of the fast family meals for the Day of Atonement (Yom Kippur), Chanukah, Purim, and the family seder at Passover, all contribute to the involvement of family in the religion and the peoplehood of Judaism. The observance of holy days also contributes toward dramatizing, particularly for children, some of the most important ideals of Judaism, including charity, thanksgiving, freedom, wisdom and learning, repentance, and self-sacrifice. They also have aesthetic values, such as the beauty and serenity that can come from a family Shabbat evening dinner.

The emphasis on family also occurs throughout life-cycle events in Judaism, starting with the very birth of a child, and often this is intertwined with an emphasis on the importance of deeds. For instance, one of the most important family occasions in Judaism is a boy's Bar Mitzvah or a girl's Bat Mitzvah which is celebrated when a child reaches the age of thirteen and from the standpoint of traditional Jewish law becomes an adult who can participate fully in Jewish life. Great warmth permeates the synagogue service. The interrelationship and importance of family, tradition, and deeds are illustrated in the following prayer from Gates of Prayer. It is to be read by a parent of the

Bar or Bat Mitzvah during that portion of the service in which a passage from the Torah is read or chanted:

> Into our hands, O God, You have placed Your Torah, to be held high by parents and children, and taught by one generation to the next.
>
> Whatever has befallen us, our people have remained steadfast in loyalty to the Torah. It was carried into exile in the arms of parents that their children might not be deprived of their birthright.
>
> And now I pray that you, my child, will always be worthy of this inheritance. Take its teaching into your heart, and in turn pass it on to your children and those who come after you. May you be a faithful Jew, searching for wisdom and truth, working for justice and peace. Thus will you be among those who labor to bring nearer the day when the Lord shall be One and His name shall be One.

The Concept of Peoplehood

Related to the Jewish emphasis on the family is the broader social concept of Judaism as a peoplehood, and not just a religion. The underlying foundation of Judaism is the covenant between God and the Jewish people. There is an empathic feeling among Jews and Jewish communities which flows out of the bond of Jewish peoplehood and has had many positive benefits, including concern for the care and education of children, substantial charitable commitments for homes and institutions for the care of the elderly, and concern for the welfare of other Jews, including those in other countries. The concept of peoplehood is one of the most important reasons underlying the major charitable commitments made by Jews in the Diaspora in support of Israel.[3]

---

[3] The Diaspora refers to those Jews who live outside of the State of Israel. In terms of numbers, the world Jewish community is very small — numbering approximately

A Closing Word to Part 1

Judaism is a loving, meaningful religion that in its truest ideals welcomes all. The values emphasized by Judaism, including the importance of family, the reverence and respect of children for their parents, and the emphasis on human actions in this world, bonded together by the richness of Jewish tradition such as the Shabbat evening family dinner, contribute toward the very special emotional feeling most Jews have for their Jewishness. Jewish ritual and ceremony can enhance these emotional feelings. Most Jews personalize these in individualized ways. This is particularly true in Reform Judaism, which is the most liberal branch of the Jewish religion and which affords the most freedom of personal choice in ritual matters. In Reform Judaism, there is also freedom for individuals to have varying views about God's being and existence and freedom to choose a theology for ourselves that is compatible with our own personal feelings about God and without any structured or doctrinal imposition of a theology on anyone else.

Many Jews believe that if there were a visitor from another planet who was seeking the kind of religious identification that would make the most sense from a rational standpoint and would have the most positive impact on civilization, he or she would find that Judaism would be the most appealing. If you were to add to this the emotional satisfaction, warmth, and support that come from being a part of the Jewish family — the Jewish community — with its traditions, culture, and history unique among all peoples of the earth — there is little doubt among most Jews who have experienced these feelings that there is nothing else like it in the entire world. Logically, this is understandable because there has to be something very special about Judaism to have enabled it to survive these thousands of years in the

---

three million Jews in Israel and approximately ten million Jews outside of Israel, of whom five and one-half million live in the United States and somewhat less than two million live in Russia under totalitarian Communist rule which discriminates against Jews and severely limits their freedom to practice their religion.

face of adversities and hostilities almost without precedent in human history.

Obviously, the warmth and emotional attachments underlying these feelings cannot be gained overnight. Like most good things, it takes time and effort, but the rewards of personal satisfaction and growth can be very great for both you and your family.

The brief passages of prayer in this booklet and the short references to Jewish traditions, Jewish concerns ranging from the importance of family to the importance of charity and freedom, the concept of the Jewish people, and the priority of the Jewish emphasis on deeds, study, and learning are but a tiny fraction of the riches of Judaism. If they have whetted your appetite to learn more about Judaism — the religion and the culture — and what it can mean for you; if, on the basis of what you have read thus far, you believe that there is much about Judaism that is compatible with your own personal philosophy; then, seek to learn more, for the more you learn about Judaism, the more appealing it will be and the more relevant it can become in contributing to your life and to your personal quest for happiness, including a deepening of your spiritual dimension, thereby adding greater meaning to your life. Ultimately, these are the most important personal benefits that relate to the question, "Why should I choose to be Jewish?"

This leads to the second question in this booklet: "What is Jewish Outreach and what does Jewish Outreach mean for me?" The best way to begin to answer this question is with a brief overview of the development of modern Reform Jewish Outreach.

PART 2
THE REBIRTH OF JEWISH OUTREACH

Deep biblical roots support the tradition of Jews seeking to bring others into the Jewish religion. The patriarch, Abraham, was himself a convert. Ancient Judaism taught: "When someone comes to you, draw him nigh. Do not push him away." Moses, the great Lawgiver, chose a non-Israelite as his wife. Ruth, a Moabite woman, chose Judaism with the words repeated by converts today: "Your people shall be my people, your God, my God." Her legacy was the dynasty of King David. Isaiah fervently believed in Israel's mission as a universal faith and spoke of Israel as "a light to the nations that my salvation may reach to the end of the earth." He looked to the day when the House of God would be called "a house of prayer for all peoples."

During the talmudic period, Jewish missionary efforts were so successful that in the first century the world Jewish population increased to between two and five million. However, in the fourth century the Edict of Constantine established Christianity as the official state religion and made conversion to Judaism a capital offense. Conversion efforts therefore temporarily ceased, but they resumed in medieval times. Then, in the late fifteenth century when the Spanish Inquisition reinstituted capital punishment for the "crime" of conversion to Judaism, together with the doctrine of "heresy," Jewish conversion efforts ceased and the rabbis developed a tradition of discouraging converts. This post-Inquisition development has led many more traditional Jews to assume erroneously that Judaism does not welcome converts, when in fact there were major periods of Jewish history when Judaism was a proselytizing religion.

Considering that the Jewish people have survived for nearly 4,000 years without a homeland for much of that time, their survival is perhaps the most miraculous in history. Scholars may differ on which factors were the most important in enabling the Jewish people to survive, but the fact remains that the tradition of the covenant with God and the laws, values, and other traditions of the Jewish religion emanating out of the Torah have been key elements contributing to the survival of Judaism and the Jewish people. Sometimes the literal language in various passages of the Bible, the Talmud, and other ancient writings seems harsh by twentieth-century standards. But the key to Jewish survival has been that, in comparison to the other contemporary societies at any particular time, Jewish teachings and writings, taken as a whole, with their emphasis on one God for all humankind, laws and deeds rather than faith, love of humankind, and the importance of family and education, have had very positive influences on Jews and have sustained the Jewish people.

The American
Jewish Experience

One of the best examples of the positive influence of Judaism on Jews is its beneficial impact on America's political, economic, and cultural life. American Jews have made important contributions toward safeguarding the inalienable constitutional rights of citizens and helping our country expand the economic opportunities of all Americans. In the fields of human rights and social justice, Jews have been called "America's conscience" and have played major roles in important progressive changes in our society. This is a natural outgrowth of the ethical concerns of Judaism and the emphasis of Judaism on human action.

Moreover, in education, government, law, medicine, the natural sciences, social sciences, and the arts Jews have made outstanding achievements far beyond that which might be expected from their relatively small numbers. These accomplishments have benefited our entire nation. When perceptive non-Jewish leaders are asked to comment on what it would be like in the United States without the American Jewish community, the response is often that it would be "a terrible loss" if America did not have the participation and leadership of American Jews in civic affairs, charitable endeavors, and in the sciences and the arts.[4]

America, in general, and the American Jewish community, in particular, have benefited from the openness of American society and the opportunities for Jews to excel in many fields. On the other hand, the breakdown of religious barriers and the increasing acceptance of Jews by non-Jews have led to a problem of immense consequence to many Jews: accelerating assimilation. Perhaps the best evidence of the acceptance of Jews by non-Jews is the fact that more than one-third of all marriages of Jews involve one partner who was not born Jewish. (A recent study in Denver indicated an intermarriage rate of more than 60 percent.)

Recent studies also indicate that, in the case of an interfaith marriage (more commonly known by Jews as a "mixed marriage" where one of the partners at the time of the marriage is Jewish and one is not), the non-Jewish partner would often choose Judaism as his or her religion, if asked. Yet, in many cases, they simply have not been asked to choose Judaism. Studies also have shown that converts to Judaism tend to make stronger commitments to Judaism in such areas as attendance at religious services and observance of home rituals and holiday observances than the population of born Jews as a whole. Many converts have indicated that their reason for conversion was one

---

[4] Much has been written about Jews who have achieved preeminence in fields ranging from the concert stage to the frontiers of medical research, such as the development of polio vaccine. Perhaps the single most impressive statistic is that, although Jews comprise less than three percent of the population, more than twenty percent of American Nobel Prize winners have been Jews.

of serious, intrinsic intent. They feel Judaism is a strong and meaningful faith. Perhaps most important of all from a long-range standpoint, the overwhelming majority of Jews by choice believe it to be very important for every Jewish child to receive a continuing Jewish education.[5]

There is no doubt that Judaism is unique and has much to offer to humankind. More and more Jews have come to recognize this as the problems of the world have become more complex and the very survival of humanity is threatened. Accordingly, there has been a rebirth of interest in considering whether Judaism should return to its biblical heritage and let the people of the world know that Judaism is a vital, vibrant religion that has much to contribute to society and to the peace and happiness of men and women, and that anyone who chooses to do so can become a Jew.

Demographic Factors and Jewish Outreach

We Jews are optimistic. Despite all of the hardships and suffering that our people have endured from our slavery in Egypt to the genocide of Hitler, we believe that men and women can work together in peace to build a better world. Indeed, our optimism has been one of the main ingredients underlying the miraculous survival of the Jewish people for these thousands of years.

Yet, despite our innate optimism, there is one area of increasing concern that hangs like a sword of Damocles over all of us, and that is the diminishing Jewish population throughout the world in general and in North America in particular. The combination of a low birthrate of between 1.6 and 1.7 children per Jewish family coupled with an intermarriage rate approaching 50 percent have led demogra-

---

[5] From *New Jews, the Dynamics of Religious Conversion,* Steven Huberman, Union of American Hebrew Congregations, 1979.

phers to a horrifying conclusion: Over the next seventy-five years the number of Jews in the United States and Canada could dwindle from the present figures of around five and one-half million to around one or two million, or even less.

What would it be like for the remaining remnant of Jews to be such a small minority? What effect would the lack of a significant Jewish minority have on the United States? And what would the impact of these circumstances be on the world Jewish community in general and on Israel in particular?

Although there is not universal agreement among demographic experts on the exact numbers, the prevailing view is clear. If present trends continue, the number of Jews seventy-five years from now could constitute substantially less than one-half of one percent of the total population in America.

In light of these facts, many thoughtful Jews have been exploring the concept of Jewish Outreach from a second perspective: They have become increasingly concerned about the survival of Judaism in the face of the murder of six million Jewish men, women, and children by the Nazis and in the face of these very adverse demographic trends within the North American Jewish community. People might argue whether it might take less than seventy-five years or perhaps somewhat longer before the American Jewish population becomes less than one million. But the great majority of demographic experts do not argue about the inexorable trend. Many people believe this is bad for both Jews and non-Jews in light of the tremendous contributions that Jews have made to the United States and Canada and in light of the unique perspective of Judaism from the rational aspect of its emphasis on this world and human actions to the emotional warmth and satisfaction that Judaism can bring to those who embrace it.

Some individuals believe that, apart from encouraging an increase in the birthrate for Jewish families, the primary solution to this problem lies in better programs of Jewish education, including summer Jewish camping experiences, which lead to greater religious commitment. However, in communities across the country, there are young Jewish adults who have received a good Jewish education but have intermarried and joined the increasing numbers of unaffiliated Jews. Perceptive Jewish leaders are becoming increasingly aware that, in America's open society, Jewish education alone is not enough. There must be something *in addition* to Jewish education. The most natural and logical program to consider is a return by Jews to their historical traditions, reaching out to non-Jews — particularly those married to Jews and the children of those interfaith marriages who might not have been raised as Jews — in the hope that they might consider the possibility of choosing Judaism. (Of course, reaching out is in substance an educational endeavor.)

But, as soon as one enters upon this path, one is faced with the question: Why should a program of Jewish Outreach be limited to those who are married to Jews or are contemplating marriage to a Jew or to those who might have a Jewish parent or grandparent but have not been raised as Jews?

Albert Einstein said that he was sorry that he was born a Jew, because it denied him the opportunity of choosing Judaism. Should not Jews let others know that Judaism is an open society and that for those people not identified with any particular religion, who may be searching for a religion compatible with their own personal philosophy, Judaism is an alternative to consider?

The Adoption
of Jewish Outreach
by Reform Judaism

Many of these factors helped set the stage for a historic address by Rabbi Alexander Schindler, president of the Union of American Hebrew Congregations (UAHC), on December 2, 1978, before the UAHC Board of Trustees. In that dramatic address Rabbi Schindler called for the return of Jews to their biblical tradition of Jewish Outreach. The trustees immediately responded and directed that a special Outreach Task Force be appointed, and the Central Conference of American Rabbis (CCAR) joined in the overall study. Over the following two and one-half years, issues were explored and debated in the traditions of Judaism. That study, which culminated in a formal written report of the Task Force to the 1981 UAHC Biennial Convention, ultimately led to the birth of a Jewish Outreach program in the United States and Canada.

There is an old story among Jews that, whenever two Jews get together discussing matters involving religion or politics, there are always three different opinions. Perhaps the most remarkable aspect of the work of the Task Force is that ultimately the twenty-six members, nine of whom were rabbis, were able to arrive at a unanimous consensus.

Five resolutions were proposed calling for programs of Reform Jewish Outreach: (1) "to meet the special needs of the non-Jewish partner" in an interfaith marriage, "to welcome these individuals into the community" and into the synagogue, enhance the Jewish content of their family life, encourage them to raise their children as Jews, and to choose Judaism as their own personal faith; (2) to meet the needs of children of interfaith marriages, to provide them with "experiential opportunities enabling them to more fully understand and appreciate the quality of Jewish life and the heritage of the Jewish people," encourage them to enroll in programs of Jewish education, and upon reaching college and young adult age "to freely choose Judaism as their personal faith"; (3) to meet the needs of an increasing number of people seeking information about Introduction to Judaism courses, including individuals considering conversion to Judaism; (4) to meet the needs of people who have recently chosen Judaism as their religion and help them in their transition into the synagogue and the general Jewish community; and (5) to communicate to Americans of no religious preference "information about the history, traditions, beliefs, and values of Judaism — that Judaism is a loving, meaningful, spiritual religion that welcomes all who wish to embrace it" — so that, in the event they are seeking religious identification, they consider Judaism as one of their alternatives.

These five resolutions were enthusiastically adopted by the 3,000 delegates to the 1981 UAHC Biennial Convention. There were several reasons why the proposed program of Reform Jewish Outreach struck such a responsive chord among those representatives of the liberal branch of the American Jewish community. Most important was the recognition of how many people have been directly or indirectly touched by the questions raised in considering Jewish Outreach: people with sons and daughters, nieces and nephews, or children of close friends who had married persons who had chosen to become Jewish and persons who had not chosen to become Jewish. The opportunities afforded by programs reaching out to welcome people who have recently chosen to become Jews and to those partners in marriage who have not chosen to become Jews, encouraging them to raise their children as Jews, were all areas with which born Jews could identify. They could also identify with the need for programs directed toward the parents of the Jewish partner in an interfaith marriage to help these parents in what is often a very emotionally upsetting situation, with one of the goals being that their grandchildren would be raised as Jews.

There was also widespread recognition of the need for Judaism to reach out to the children of interfaith marriages. Many of these children have been raised with no religious identity. They should have an opportunity to understand the history and the meaning of the religion of their Jewish parent. There was also enthusiastic support for improving the content of Introduction to Judaism courses which are being offered in greater numbers across the country.

In addition, many delegates to that convention were themselves Jews by choice and recognized the positive benefits of such a program for themselves and their families. There was also recognition of the increasing desire on the part of many non-Jews searching for religious identity to enroll in Introduction to Judaism courses, even though they may not be considering marriage to a Jewish person.

All of these are areas of first priority, and, although the resources available to the Union of American Hebrew Congregations are unfortunately inadequate to meet the need, work is already underway to implement Reform Jewish Outreach programs in each of these areas to the extent of the limited resources available.

Furthermore, once Jewish Outreach programs are underway in these four areas of first priority, particularly in the area of outreach to the children of interfaith marriages of college and young adult age, there will be a natural future transition into the area of outreach to the religiously nonpreferenced. This transition will be easily made and more readily accepted as people actually see the positive aspects of dignified, educational Jewish Outreach programing already underway in the initial four areas.

Collateral Benefits of Jewish Outreach

Another important aspect of a program of Jewish Outreach is the tremendous collateral benefits that such a program can have upon unaffiliated Jews. In the words of the 1981 Report of the Jewish Outreach Task Force:

> A dignified, sensitively prepared informational program about Judaism would be heard by all Americans, including unaffiliated Jews who may be inspired to return to a more active identification with Judaism. It would also be heard by other Americans who may have no desire to consider choosing Judaism as their religion but who nevertheless would gain an understanding about Judaism that would help dispel myth and suspicion.
>
> Such an undertaking, if done properly, would have great impact upon born Jews, particularly those who are ambivalent about their own Jewishness. Jewish college students, so often assailed by missionaries and representatives of cults and charismatic movements, will learn that Judaism is a faith that attracts countless young people like themselves who have found fulfillment in its practices. Higher rates of synagogue affiliation, greater interest in books of Jewish content, and more positive Jewish identification may well be collateral benefits accruing from this project.

There are other potential collateral benefits, such as the impetus of Jewish Outreach on Jews to travel to and study in Israel and reidentify with the land in which their religious heritage is rooted. For those Jews who seek to have their children marry other Jewish persons and raise a family, there is another major benefit of Jewish Outreach and that is the fact that a Jewish individual is more likely to marry another Jewish individual if the total Jewish population in North America is five million or more, as compared to one million or less.

This leads into a related area: The assertion by some more traditional Jews that numbers are not important and that the world would be better off with 500,000 deeply committed Jews rather than five million Jews. I disagree because I believe we can have both and, indeed, more. Concurrently with programs of Jewish Outreach we should work to enhance the spiritual quality and educational participation of North American Jews in Jewish life. There is nothing to lose and very much to gain in striving toward both goals, and as a practical matter there is a far greater likelihood of having a significant number of committed Jews if we have the strength and resources of a Jewish population base of five or six million rather than a mere half million.

Finally, some people have urged concentrating on seeking the return of unaffiliated Jews before reaching out to converts. Reform Judaism has concluded that neither of these is exclusive of the other. Mutual benefits would accrue from Jewish Outreach programs designed to do both, and in fact we are already seeing that born Jews are "coming back" as a result of the initial Jewish Outreach efforts that are underway.

Differences in Jewish Outreach

It is important to understand some basic differences between programs of Reform Jewish Outreach as compared with programs of other religions which are called "Outreach" or which have proselytizing aspects to them. The representatives of Reform Judaism have agreed that any program of Jewish Outreach should seek only to attract people not affiliated with any other religion. This is in contrast to the evangelical efforts of most other groups who seek converts, regardless of whether they identify with another faith. Also, any program of Reform Jewish Outreach will avoid an aggressive approach, such as other groups practice on street corners or airport lobbies. It will instead be directed toward letting the world know about the true meaning and religious values of Judaism and also letting the world know that there are no barriers to entry into the Jewish religion and that, if a person of no religious preference is exploring various choices, Judaism is one of the alternatives to consider.

Outreach as a Permanent Program of Reform Judaism

In November, 1983, a major new step in Jewish Outreach was inaugurated, concurrently with the completion of the work of the Outreach Task Force. A permanent joint Outreach Commission was formed by the UAHC and the CCAR as an integral part of the American Jewish community and as a major agenda item for the Reform movement. The new commission will not only contribute to the growth and development of Jewish Outreach programs among all Reform Jewish congregations in the United States and Canada, but it will seek to encourage the other main branches of Judaism to develop appropriate, dignified Jewish Outreach programs of their own. An ever-increasing number of Jewish leaders have endorsed the concept of Jewish Outreach.

Obviously, sensitive, effective programs of Jewish Outreach will have a very important impact on the demographic trends within the American Jewish community. The return of the Jewish people to their historic traditions of outreach will have a substantial effect on the ability of the American Jewish community to maintain its proportionate population at the two and one-half to five percent level rather than a one percent level or less. Thus, the degree of success of Jewish Outreach may determine if the United States and Canada will continue to benefit from a vibrant North American Jewish community in the twenty-first century and beyond.

Of greatest importance, however, are not just the numbers of Jews or their contributions to society. Rather, the central benefit of Jewish Outreach is the impact of Judaism on the life of the individual in terms of learning, worship, personal faith, and happiness, and in terms of the values and deeds by which women and men conduct their lives.

Concluding Comments

I have five children, all of whom have received a Jewish education, including Bar and Bat Mitzvahs. They have also all visited Israel — the four oldest on high school summer Jewish programs. Many people say that it is "tough to be a Jew" because we live in a society which still has a lot of underlying prejudice against Jews. Nevertheless, I want my children to be informed, participating Jews. Why? Because I believe that Judaism is a wonderful religion that brings out the best in humanity and offers to all of us as individuals an infinite amount of wisdom and support for our daily lives.

Inherent in the tradition of Judaism is the optimistic belief that people and society are perfectible. Although this belief is rooted in thousands of years of Jewish history and tradition, it has never been more relevant and more needed than at the present time.

I believe in the centrality of the synagogue and Jewish education to Jewish survival. For this reason I have included in this booklet brief selections from the New Reform Prayer Book as well as from the ancient *Ethics of the Fathers*. It is my firm conviction that Jewish Outreach is also an essential element of Jewish survival. Outreach is a crucial catalyst to help bring unaffiliated Jews and interfaith married couples into the synagogue and to encourage people in interfaith relationships to learn more about Judaism and enroll in Introduction to Judaism courses. This, in turn, will help lead them and their children into the synagogue and into programs of enriched Jewish education.

Judaism is not just a religion; it is also a community and a culture which encourage particular warmth and closeness among Jews. That is why the historic resolutions on Jewish Outreach adopted by the Union of American Hebrew Congregations include such phrases as welcoming the non-Jewish partner in an interfaith marriage "into the community" and providing individuals of interfaith marriage background with information and "experiential opportunities enabling them to understand and appreciate more fully the quality of Jewish life and the heritage of the Jewish people."

For me, the philosophy and teachings of Judaism and the people-hood of Judaism have made me realize how fortunate I was to be born into a Jewish family and have reinforced my belief that in this age, when there are so many choices that individuals have, I want to continue to choose to be Jewish. Therefore, in a sense, I, too, consider myself to be a Jew by choice.

Ultimately, what Jewish Outreach means for you and for all men and women depends upon how well we understand and appreciate the philosophy, teachings, and beauty of the Jewish religion and culture and how it can positively affect our lives. Therefore, it is appropriate in ending this exploration of Jewish Outreach and the question, "Why should I choose to be Jewish?" to turn once again to a Jewish prayer. A personal favorite of mine is a meditation from one of the alternative Friday evening Shabbat services in *Gates of Prayer:*

> In this quiet hour of worship we reflect upon the meaning of our lives.
>
> I harbor within — we all do — a vision of my highest self, a dream of what I could and should become. May I pursue this vision, labor to make real my dream. Thus will I give meaning to my life.
>
> An artist in the course of painting will pause, lay aside the brush, step back from the canvas, and consider what needs to

be done, what direction to be taken. So does each of us on this Sabbath eve pause to reflect. As I hope to make my life a work of art, so may this hour of worship help me to turn back to the canvas of life to paint the portrait of my highest self.

May my efforts to grow in moral stature bring me the joy of achievement. And may I always hold before my eyes the vision of perfection we call by the name of God — and grow toward Him. (Shabbat Service II)

Note about the Author. David Belin has served as chairman of the Union of American Hebrew Congregations Outreach Program from its inception in 1978. In December, 1983, he was named to head the permanent UAHC/CCAR Commission on Outreach, successor body to the Reform movement's Task Force on Reform Jewish Outreach. He also serves as vice chairman of the Board of Trustees of the UAHC and as chairman of the North American Board of the World Union for Progressive Judaism. In addition he has had a broad range of public service including appointment by Chief Justice Earl Warren as counsel to the President's Commission on the Assassination of President Kennedy (Warren Commission), appointment by President Ford as executive director of the Commission on CIA Activities within the United States (Rockefeller Commission), and current membership on the President's Committee for the Arts and Humanities.